TRANSPORT IN MY COMMUNITY

TRUCKS AND LORRIES

by Cari Meister

raintree

a Capstone company — publishers for children

Lorries and trucks do lots of different jobs.
They are big and powerful.

BRRRUMM! BRRRUMM!

Lorries have been around
for more than 100 years.

At first they had steam engines.

Today, lorries and trucks run on fuel. Some use diesel. Some use petrol.

The driver fills up the tank.

Time to go!

Here comes an articulated lorry.
The driver sits in the cab at the front.
The cab is above the engine.

The driver fills up the tank.

Time to go!

Some trucks are just for fun. Monster trucks are huge. They can do stunts.

CRASH!

CRUNCH

They drive over cars with their
massive wheels. People like to watch!

Here comes an articulated lorry.
The driver sits in the cab at the front.
The cab is above the engine.

HONK!

HONK!

Articulated lorries have long trailers. They carry food and goods across the country.

Rubbish lorries collect rubbish. They pick up bins and empty them into the back of the lorry.

The rubbish gets squashed in the back of the lorry. It will be taken to a rubbish and recycling centre.

A dumper truck drives up to a digger.
The digger fills the truck's bed with soil.
The dumper truck drives away.
Then it tilts its bed to empty the soil.

A car transporter takes cars from place to place. The driver lowers the back of the transporter. Then the cars drive up onto the lorry. The cars are taken away to be sold.

Lunchtime!

Food trucks are like cafés on wheels. They have cookers and fridges on board.

YUM! YUM!

Time to eat!

Which truck will clear all that snow from the road?

The snowplough!

Snowploughs have strong blades for pushing snow. Ploughs make clear paths for cars. Then the cars can travel along the road.

This car has broken down.

A tow truck comes to help.

The car is hooked onto the truck.
The truck tows the car away to be fixed.

A siren blares. Lights flash.

NEE-NAH! NEE-NAH!

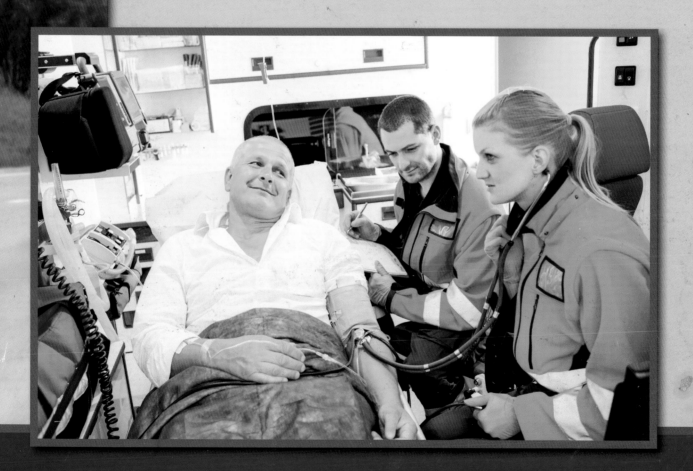

Ambulances pick up poorly or injured people.
They rush them to hospital.

Oh no!

A building is on fire. Here comes a fire engine. Fire engines carry hoses, long ladders and other rescue equipment.

WHOOSH!

Firefighters use the hoses to put out the fire. They use the ladders to rescue people from tall buildings.

Trucks and lorries help people do all kinds of jobs. They carry food and take away rubbish. They clear snow and rescue people in trouble.

You could drive a truck one day!

Timeline

1800s

The first trucks carry goods from factories to trains.

1929

Lillie McGee Drennan becomes the first official female truck driver.

1939

Fredrick Jones gets a patent for a truck air-conditioning system. This keeps food cool during transport.

2013

The Belaz 75710 is introduced. It's the largest mining dumper truck in the world.

1880

1900

1920

1940

1960

1980

2000

2020

1895

Karl Benz builds the first truck that runs on petrol.

1899

The first articulated lorry is sold in the United States.

1970s

The CB radio becomes a popular way for lorry drivers to communicate with each other.

2016

A self-driving lorry carries goods for the first time in history.

Glossary

articulated lorry type of lorry that has two parts – the front with the engine, and a trailer for carrying things

bed the back end of a truck; the bed tips to empty loads

blade the wide part of the front of a truck that pushes snow or soil

communicate to share information, thoughts or feelings

diesel a heavy fuel that burns to make power; many lorries run on diesel fuel

engine a machine that makes the power needed to move something

hydrant a large pipe with a valve that draws water from the city's water supply

trailer part of a lorry that carries goods

Find out more

Lorries (Transport), Mari Shuh (Raintree, 2018)

Monster Trucks (Mighty Machines). Ian Graham (QED Publishing, 2009)

Rescue! (Big Machines), Catherine Veitch (Raintree, 2015)

Websites

www.explainthatstuff.com/ firefighting.html
Find out more about amazing fire engines!

www.sciencekids.co.nz/ sciencefacts/vehicles.html
Check out this website for fun facts about different types of transport.

Index

Raintree is an imprint of Capstone Global Library Limited, a company incorporated in England and Wales having its registered office at 264 Banbury Road, Oxford, OX2 7DY – Registered company number: 6695582

www.raintree.co.uk
myorders@raintree.co.uk

Text © Capstone Global Library Limited 2020
The moral rights of the proprietor have been asserted.

Editor: Michelle Parkin
Designer: Rachel Tesch
Printed and bound in India

ISBN: 978 1 4747 6881 8 (hardback)   ISBN 978 1 4747 6901 3 (paperback)

British Library Cataloguing in Publication Data
A full catalogue record for this book is available from the British Library.

Acknowledgements
Dreamstime: Gorgios, 8-9; Getty Images: Heritage Images, 4-5, 30 (top left), Mike Raabe, 30 (bottom right), Universal History Archive/UIG, 30 (top right); iStockphoto: HelpingHandPhotos, 13, kali9, 28, kozmoat98, 16-17, Nirian, 7, NoDerog, 18-19, Pixelci, 6, poco_bw, 26, saje, 20, shaunl, 21, 27, valentinrussanov, 19 (inset); Shutterstock: Africa Studio, 12, 29, CandyBox Images, 25 (inset), Christophe Testi, cover (top), 1, IM_photo, cover (bottom left), Krivosheev Vitaly, cover (bottom right), LadyPhotos, 5, (inset), LeitWolf, 30 (bottom left), Mikadun, 22-23, OgnjenO, cover (bottom middle), 24, PATIWIT HONGSANG, 23 (inset), TFoxFoto, 14-15, 15 (inset), Timofeev Sergey, 2-3, Vitpho, 10-11, 16 (inset)

Every effort has been made to contact copyright holders of material reproduced in this book. Any omissions will be rectified in subsequent printings if notice is given to the publisher.

All the internet addresses (URLs) given in this book were valid at the time of going to press. However, due to the dynamic nature of the internet, some addresses may have changed, or sites may have changed or ceased to exist since publication. While the author and publisher regret any inconvenience this may cause readers, no responsibility for any such changes can be accepted by either the author or the publisher.